INDIA
MODERN

INDIA
MODERN

MICHAEL FREEMAN

TUTTLE PUBLISHING
Boston • Rutland, Vermont • Tokyo

First published in the United States in 2005 by Tuttle Publishing, an imprint of Periplus Editions (HK) Ltd., with editorial offices at 153 Milk Street, Boston, Massachusetts 02109.

Originally published in Great Britain in 2005 by Mitchell Beazley, an imprint of Octopus Publishing Group, 2-4 Heron Quays, London E14 4JP

Library of Congress Cataloging-in-Publication Data is available.
ISBN 0-7946-5020-1
Distributed by:

North America, Latin America & Europe
Tuttle Publishing
364 Innovation Drive
North Clarendon, VT 05759-9436
Tel: (802) 773-8930
Fax: (802) 773-6993
info@tuttlepublishing.com
www.tuttlepublishing.com

Japan
Tuttle Publishing
Yaekari Building, 3rd Floor
5-4-12 Ōsaki
Shinagawa-ku
Tokyo 141 0032
Tel: (03) 5437-0171
Fax: (03) 5437-0755
tuttle-sales@gol.com

Asia Pacific
Berkeley Books Pte. Ltd.
130 Joo Seng Road
#06-01/03 Olivine Building
Singapore 368357
Tel: (65) 6280-1330
Fax: (65) 6280-6290
inquiries@periplus.com.sg
www.periplus.com

First edition
09 08 07 06 05   10 9 8 7 6 5 4 3 2 1

Set in The Mix

Color reproduction by Sang Choy International Pte Ltd., Hong Kong
Printed and bound in China by Toppan Printing Company Ltd.

Commissioning Editor **Anna Sanderson**
Senior Editor **Peter Taylor**
Executive Art Editor **Auberon Hedgecoe**
Design **DW Design**
Production **Gary Hayes**
Copy-editor **Ann Hildyard**
Proofreader **Kim Richardson**
Indexer **Sue Farr**

TUTTLE PUBLISHING ® is a registered trademark of Tuttle Publishing.

Contents

Introduction
The New Designers

THE TIMELINE OF INDIA'S ARCHITECTURE AND DESIGN IS ODDLY COMPRESSED. SOME FIVE THOUSAND YEARS OF INDIGENOUS STYLES, DATING BACK TO AT LEAST THE INDUS VALLEY CITIES OF 2,500 TO 1,000 BC, WERE INTERRUPTED BY A CENTURY OF COLONIAL IDEAS, THEN FOLLOWED BY HALF A CENTURY OF A MAINLY ROUGH-AND-READY INTERNATIONAL STYLE, AND NOW, WITHIN ONLY THE LAST DECADE, A DISTINCTIVE MODERN INDIAN VOICE IS FINALLY BEING HEARD. THIS IS AN EXPRESSION THAT IS CONSCIOUS BOTH OF ITS PLACE IN GLOBAL CULTURE AND OF TRADITIONAL FORMS.

Essential to an understanding of the newly emerging talents and ideas is the weight of what Vikram Bhatt and Peter Scriver in *After the Masters* call "the remarkable presence of the past in modern India". As they elaborate, "Ritual, religion and living craft traditions descend from a cultural heritage of genius and beauty ... perennial sources of inspiration to architects who attempt to embody identity and meaning in the design of new buildings." This persists in a number of ways, not always evident at first glance. The *shilpa-shastras* are the ancient collective treatises on architecture that meld the esoteric, religious and mystical components. They treat the construction of buildings in a broad and symbolic sense, with emphasis on, for example, auspicious times to begin and on the significance of the eight cardinal directions (which suggest the placement of main entrances, kitchen, bathroom and so on). Linked to this are the ritual needs of a house, such as those connected to the threshold and entrance; niches and auspicious symbols are just two of the ways in which the element of entry is defined.

The past also makes itself felt in the hand-built nature of most construction. Although a challenge when architects are looking for mechanical precision, it also invests buildings with what has been described as "a visceral quality of execution". The Indian crafts base, from stone masonry to unique local decorative techniques, is huge and readily available.

When combined with the practical influences of a hot climate, extended families, and communal society, these traditions have resulted in distinctive traditional models for dwellings. The most widespread is the *haveli*, which is essentially a courtyard house embedded in a closely packed urban neighbourhood, or *mohalla*. Courtyards provide coolness and privacy for the family, and are typically surrounded by a cloister-like *passal*, protected from outside view by either a kind of baffle or a dog-leg inner entrance. Other adaptations to heat are the *chhajja*, an overhanging canopy that shades the wall, and the *jali*, or perforated screen, as used in the *zharookha*, a projecting screened balcony. These and many others are traditional but practical elements, and modern interpretations of them are still being invented.

The colonial period of the Raj brought a different aesthetic, and during the 19th century it made itself felt in two ways. One was the introduction of a European style of living, more or less the inverse of the traditional *haveli*. Instead of an open space at the heart of a building that was joined to others in a dense urban neighbourhood, there was a detached building in the middle of a private open space – a villa or a more modest bungalow (from the Bengali – *bangla* – cottage, taken out of its context). The premier example of this is in the "colonies" of New Delhi, the city designed by Edwin Lutyens and Herbert Baker and built between 1911 and 1931. Lutyens' public buildings followed the second kind of colonial intervention – a revival of Indian architectural forms according to a British point of view. This was by no means authentic, and involved borrowing elements from other parts of the Empire as well as from the regions of India; it fell under the title "Indo-Saracenic", or just "Saracenic".

Little wonder that with Independence came a reaction to "Indianized" buildings. Modernism, and in particular the International Style, appealed, even though precision in execution was difficult using labour-intensive, non-mechanized building methods. But what made 1950s and 1960s Modernism so influential in India was the arrival of Le Corbusier and his plans for the new capital of the Punjab, Chandigarh, where work began in 1951. A generation of Indian architects, notably Balkrishna Doshi and Charles Correa who were part of the Chandigarh team, subscribed first to the Corbusier idiom and then, from 1962, to that of another Western master, Louis Kahn, whose most famous work was the all-brick Indian Institute of Management at Ahmedabad.

Yet the brave new world of post-Independent architecture and design ultimately had the effect of delaying the development of a modern Indian identity that incorporated Indian traditions. It took until the 1990s for this to work its way through, and a major stimulus was the long-awaited start of an economic boom, encouraged by the liberalizing reforms that began in 1991. The growth of an affluent middle class has always been necessary for progress in the areas of design that relate to lifestyle, and this is now happening in India.

In addition, tourism has had a special kind of influence. Visitors want an "authentic" Indian experience that will accord with a largely romantic image – the area where Raj meets Rajput, a *Far Pavilions* world of fabulous palaces and colonial empire. On the face of it this

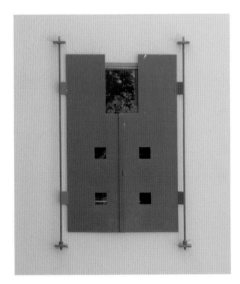

might sound to be a retrograde step for design, but in reality resort tourism in India offers the opportunity to restore and to build on a large, imaginative scale to high standards, both aesthetically and functionally. And these modern palaces are every bit as much enjoyed by the Indian middle class as by the Western and Asian. In order to flourish, design needs healthy disposable incomes, and tourism helps to tap these.

A new generation of architects, interior designers, product designers, painters, and sculptors is looking for forms that are both modern and unique – an identity that is distinctly Indian and strikes a balance, on the one hand avoiding becoming submerged in international movements, on the other escaping the conservatism of the expected and traditional. On the following pages are 40 buildings and interiors built or restored within the last eight years. This is design in progress, the beginning of a distinct period in creativity in India. Art plays a vital role in much of it, and the combination is an expression of what it is to be both Indian and modern.

Chapter 1
A Break with Tradition

MODERNISM IS RELATIVELY NEW TO INDIA. THE REASONS FOR THIS SPRING ULTIMATELY FROM THE ENORMOUS DEPTH OF CULTURAL TRADITION IN INDIA: ITS HISTORY OF ACCUMULATED KNOWLEDGE, TEACHING, AND BELIEF IS POSSIBLY THE RICHEST AND OLDEST IN THE WORLD. THE VEDAS (THE PRIMARY SACRED TEXTS OF HINDUISM) STILL INFORM MANY AREAS OF MODERN LIFE, INCLUDING – PERHAPS SURPRISINGLY TO A WESTERN AUDIENCE – ARCHITECTURE AND DESIGN.

Such an embedded belief system is not easily overturned, even in what might seem to be relatively superficial areas such as the choice of décor and the organization of space in an apartment. In addition, as the brief history of modern architecture and interior design outlined in the introduction has shown, there is a real sense of design innovation having been on hold for a few decades. This situation is now changing and, as is often the case, the pace of new ideas has been rapid and there is a strong urge to do things differently. The new generation of designers, architects, and artists (as we'll see, modern Indian art is playing a significant and constructive role in the new living spaces) is making up for lost time. Many spaces that are taken for granted in the West, such as restaurants, bars, and second holiday homes, are not at all a part of traditional Indian culture. Yet the same changes in India's economy and society that are stimulating new design ideas are also helping to create different kinds of space in which these ideas can be applied. And in India creativity has not meant simply becoming international. All of the architectural and design talent featured here has taken the more difficult but rewarding task of interpreting Modernism in a context that draws on social, artistic, and sometimes religious references, staying true to the huge and complex entity that is Indian culture.

INTEGRATING HOME AND ART

Previous spread: **In a country estate located in New Delhi's Farmlands region, a tall narrow staircase leads down from the upper entrance to the main living and dining area, interrupted by a plinth supporting a tall, modern Indian pot.**

Above: **In one of the dining-rooms, with views out over the gardens at the back of the house, the long, sinuous teak table itself is partly sculpture, one end wrapped in a design by Anupam. The large ball sculpture in the corner is constructed from stainless steel milk cans by sculptor Subodh Gupta.**

Built in 1997 by architect Inni Chatterjee, with interior design work by Samiir Wheaton, the family house of Lekha and Ranjan Poddar with their son Anupam on the outskirts of Delhi makes a strong statement both in terms of the arrangement of its space and in its use of materials. More than this, the variety of rooms is used specifically to showcase the Poddars' informed collection of modern Indian works of art, which includes paintings, sculptures, and installations. The plan features projecting wings alternating with bays, and the liberal use of plate-glass windows and doors at each end of the principal communal rooms ensures the flow of light into a structure that is predominantly stone and concrete. Most of the rooms look out onto a courtyard, terrace, or garden and the three storeys are arranged as three interconnected but separately functioning apartments so that the three members of the family can each have a measure of independence.

The use of materials, which is both confident and often unexpected, together with strong horizontal design elements breaking through interior and exterior, carries a hint of Frank Lloyd Wright's work. The unpainted walls vary from room to room, with both exposed concrete and stone playing a major part. The concrete bricks were cast on site (as we'll see in other houses, it is common practice in India to prepare building materials on the spot). In one room, concrete blocks alternate with thin horizontal bands of grit-wash, while in the bathrooms, a similar arrangement is executed in grey granite separated by thinner bands of flecked brown marble from Verona. Chatterjee plays tricks of reversal with the materials: the pairing of concrete floor and wooden ceiling in one room is reversed in another with a wooden floor and concrete ceiling, the latter cast in wooden forms.

With projects such as Devi Garh (*see* pages 68–73), her own houses, and her commissions of modern art, Lekha Poddar plays a notable part in the country's modern art, architecture, and design movements. The scale of the house and the size of its rooms have made it possible to incorporate large and striking works of art that would normally be displayed only in a public or commercial art gallery. These include two life-size fibreglass sculptures of note – a pink cow on a candy-striped oversize mattress by Subodh Gupta, and Bharti Kher's *I've seen an elephant fly*, a baby elephant completely covered with *bindi*, the traditional, tiny, stick-on decorations worn by Indian women and girls on their foreheads.

Below: **A second dining-room, with concrete brick walls and a teak ceiling, is dominated by a large fibreglass head covered in gold leaf by Ravinder Reddy. It represents Radha, consort of Krishna, but a passing resemblance to a certain south Indian politician has been noted.**

Following spread: **The upstairs living-room, also with cast concrete brick walls with grit bands, is the setting for Subodh Gupta's life-size pink fibreglass sacred cow. The painting of Mahatma Gandhi by Atul Dodya was exhibited at the Tate Modern in 2001.**

Opposite page: **In one of the bedrooms, a life-size sculpture of a baby elephant marches across the floor, lit by the row of thin, vertical, wood-shuttered windows. By artist Bharti Kher, the elephant is completely covered in** *bindi* **– the mass-produced decorative dots placed on women's foreheads. Kher relates these** *bindi* **to both fashion accessory and male sperm as a comment on India's complex gender relationships.**

Top left: **A dining-room sideboard, traditionally crafted without nails, using long wooden hinges and butterfly joints, supports a 10-centimetre (4-inch) thick black granite top.**

Top right: **An alcove in the principal living-room holds street-art terra-cotta parakeets. The undressed concrete bricks that form most interior walls in the house were cast on site.**

Left: **Three large papier-mâché masks, inspired by ceremonial forms, line the upstairs dressing-room. They are the work of Hyderabad artist C. Jagdish, who has studios both in India and in Michigan, USA.**

DISPLAY SPACE

Above: **Opening up the centre of the apartment has provided an ideal gallery space with a large wall area for hangings and several different views. On the left is a mirror-finished dish sculpture by Anish Kapoor, and on the far wall at right a painting by the Paris-based Sayad Haidar Raza.**

Right: **The kitchen echoes the spatial theme of the main living area and is organized around a central unit in stainless steel.**

Hill Park was a notable housing development of the 1950s, built on prime land on Malabar Hill, Mumbai, and designed for expatriate employees of several large British companies at a time when their commercial presence was strong in India. The several blocks are arranged in a semi-circle around a large garden, and the individual apartments are spacious and well lit from both sides of each building. The division of space, on the other hand, was in tune with the expectations of the time, with several individual rooms connected by corridors. The new owners of one apartment decided to open up the space in order to make everything except the bedrooms and bathrooms contiguous. In addition, they had a special need for which they commissioned Mumbai-based architect Bijoy Jain. This was to create a space that would function as a personal art gallery for their extensive and expanding collection of Indian modern art. The pieces, most of which are kept in storage elsewhere, are displayed in rotation, according to the owners' mood.

Previous spread: **A massive rectangular-sectioned pillar, seen here in the view from the entrance lobby, dominates the apartment structurally and visually. The 1-tonne lacquered-steel sculpture by Anish Kapoor is supported by embedded steel joists.**

Above: **New Delhi artist Mrinalini Mukherjee works with intricately knotted hemp ropes in earthy colours in forms that convey a strong sexuality through phallic shapes and mysterious folds.**

This dual requirement – living, dining, study, and kitchen areas that are interconnected and a flexible gallery space – called for a careful compromise between the removal of partitions and maximizing the wall-hanging area. A massive structural column rises through the centre of the apartment, and in the original division a wall from here to the front created two rooms with a corridor behind to the main bedroom and bathroom. Jain cut back the non-structural partitions up to the column to create a space that revolves around a central unit – ideal for a gallery. All of this was achieved in close consultation with the owners, who had firm ideas about how they wanted to live in the new space. An important decision was to keep the original Crittall windows with their 1950s industrial aesthetic (almost all other renovations in the development resulted in their replacement).

The treatment of the walls was given a high priority. They needed to be plain, offering the maximum space possible for displaying pictures, with a detailed finish, and yet also

express some character. For this, Jain turned to a traditional Rajasthani lime-plaster technique known as *araish*. Its most similar counterpart in Europe is *stucco veneziano*, but in the Rajasthani version pure lime is mixed with marble dust. This is applied in a number of thin layers. "Basically," as Jain explains, "you grind one layer into another, and you can control the texture by choosing the size of the dust particles." As each layer must dry before application of the next one, it is a time-consuming process – 14 layers were applied here. To help with the execution, Jain commissioned Kate Dineen, an English artist who gained a doctorate in the *araish* technique after studying for eight years in Rajasthan. Her skill allowed him to plan for a sharp, precise edge to corners. To further increase the precision of the walls, he used a shadow groove at the join with the floor. This "negative skirting", as Jain calls it, also allows the walls to appear to float. At the top of the wall, he inserted a second metal groove, this one facing upwards, which is used as an unobtrusive system for hanging paintings.

Above centre: **The guest bedroom features a painting by Arpita Singh, whose work typically deals with the inner world of Indian women and the space they inhabit in modern society.**

Above right: **The ensuite bathroom for the master bedroom features a single block of pale limestone carved into a double-sized washbasin.**

A NEW AESTHETIC

Below: **A large central square inset of flamed finished black granite in the wooden floor of this living-room was used to anchor the grouping of furniture, which includes a Chinese opium day-bed in the foreground. The large wall-hanging is a 17th-century Jain painting.**

New Delhi's so-called "colonies" were a post-Independence phenomenon that marked the beginning of the end of a certain Indian lifestyle. The traditional paradigm of Indian domestic architecture among the moderately affluent had been the *haveli*, an urban mansion centred on a private courtyard. This style of building accommodated a particular way of life and culture that was to disappear rapidly in favour of housing schemes modelled on European tastes. After Independence they became the preferred alternative for the relatively wealthy to the crowded, traditional, and largely communal existence in the older parts of the city, but now, decades on, most such buildings are ripe for renovation.

Friends Colony West is typical of the more exclusive of south Delhi's colonies, with large properties well separated by gardens and lawns. This first floor of a large three-storey house was one of architect and interior designer Rajiv Saini's early commissions, completed in 2000, and the first stage in a renovation that is now continuing on the ground floor. Like many large houses in India, this one was subdivided to accommodate different members of the family as their needs changed. By the time Saini came to the project, this first floor had become two apartments of 325 square metres (3,500 square feet) each. When one part of the family moved out, the owners decided to convert it into a single living space for a couple with two grown-up daughters. Practically, this meant living-room, dining-room, study, and four bedrooms (three for the family plus a guest room).

Below: **A recessed niche in one wall houses a collection of antique bronzes of various manifestations of the female goddess Devi. The colour red in Indian mythology represents the female power (*shakti*), symbolizes destruction (associated with the larger icon of the goddess Kali), and is also representative of the auspicious union of marriage (*sindoor*).**

Above: **The entrance to the first floor, accessed from an elevator at left, relies heavily for its impact on two works of art. At the far end are the double-sided paintings by Nilma Sheikh, while in the foreground is a light sculpture by Chitvanyu Majumdar, which makes a dramatic statement in its own right as well as keying the entire lobby area.**

An intense effort over two years, with the close involvement of the owner, resulted in the radical rethinking of this space, not only in the removal of walls but in a very different stylistic approach. Saini says, "So much of a project depends on interaction with clients," and this assignment in particular benefited from the time spent and from the client's commitment to working through ideas from the conceptual to the detailed finish. "It was understood that art would play a rôle," Saini continues. "The owners wanted to bring in the best art for the space and were not overly concerned about the cost of doing that. In fact, integrating the art with the spatial design was a key element of this project."

The lobby, at the lift entrance and in the centre of the floor, is the first and most striking evidence of this. Living-room, dining-room, and study all open out onto this space and works of art play a vital rôle in, as Saini puts it, "ordering them in a manner to create various overlapping scenes". Having opened up the skylight with glass bricks, Saini turned his attention to the division between the study and the lobby. At a gallery preview he saw a work in the form of a pair of double-sided painted screens by artist Nilima Sheikh, "and I knew we had to get it for the house". Hanging them with space around the margins serves to animate and energize the view from both sides, but involved taking down a 60-centimetre- (2-foot-) thick, load-bearing wall. Next to this, the wall directly underneath the skylight called for a treatment that would exploit the downlighting, and a natural solution was roughly chiselled bands of marble. The low platform below, with regularly spaced stone bowls, was designed to create a visual base for this. At the other end of the lobby, by the lift, Saini and the owners planned for an installation that would be immediately striking as soon as the lift doors were opened, and designed a triangular alcove even before finding or commissioning the work.

Left: The hand-painted textile ceiling brings warmth into an otherwise stark slate- and marble-clad bathroom. Spotlights help maximize the dramatic effect.

Left: Double-sided paintings held by clear-glass surrounds screen the lobby from this family-room. A natural palette of materials was used – rice paper on the walls, linen on the sofas, and cane matting on the ceiling.

DELHI FARMS

Above: **The corner of one of the living-rooms, with sliding glass doors giving out onto the gardens. On the wall, a square internal window provides glimpses of the circulation space beyond – hand-carved in Pondicherry from a solid, five-inch thick block of granite, this is a modern interpretation of the traditional** *jali* **perforated stone screen.**

Beginning in the 1990s, a particular kind of suburban expansion began to spread out from Delhi into the surrounding farmland, particularly in the south and west. These are, for the large part, individual developments, usually on substantial plots of land, and while for tax purposes many of the properties are called farms, they are anything but. This area has some of the city's largest and most luxurious homes, and these new constructions on open land have been an opportunity to experiment with new architectural ideas and modern interior design. The original impetus for building on farmland was the tax break on land classified as agricultural, and the first properties were usually second homes. Now, however, the very term "farm" has status, and a growing number of properties are primary residences.

Each of these three houses is, in its own way, an exemplar of a spacious, open style of domestic architecture that is relatively new to India. The "colony" style of house that evolved during the 1960s followed a Western model in abandoning the courtyard and a conventional arrangement of rooms. These "farms", on the other hand, make use of the much greater available land area, and they do it both through interior spaces that are larger and more free-flowing, and by creating a more interesting inter-penetration of house and garden. The space available on these former farmland plots, together with the lack of any necessity to complement and fit in with neighbouring properties, make this area a fertile experimental ground for new architects and designers.

In the first of the three properties, designed by Rajiv Saini, large window walls and a lavish use of different types of stone help to create spaces that are light and airy yet also monumental. The structure is, in fact, two almost identical buildings adjacent and set at an angle to each other. The reason for this was, as is commonly the case in India, that the house was to accommodate more than a single nuclear family. Each needed a measure of independence while being able to be in close contact with the other, and a short walkway between the two structures makes this possible. One result was the increase in wall area – which became an opportunity to use large picture windows. Given the owners' love of gardens, this was a logical choice, and all the rooms have an extensive view of the lawns, trees, and plants.

Below: The floor of the dining room is in a unique brownish marble, with hair-like veins of orange and red from its iron content. This colour is picked up in the red cedar used for the sideboards, ceiling and wall, and in the choice of painting, a work by Jitish Kallat exhibited in 2001 at the Tate Modern. The table was also designed by the architect.

In Saini's latest work in this area, nearby, he was given more freedom in the basic structure as well as in materials and interiors. Phase one had already begun when he became involved, with the plinth and columns in place. With minor modifications to the plan, the elevations were reworked to create a basic white cubic structure. Two skewed walls cutting into this cube emerge, defining the spine of the second half. As they pass through the structure, these spinal walls change from glass within to concrete outside and intersect the landscape, aligned to a black, polished limestone water body holding a row of five champa trees. This movement from outside to inside, combined with the vast area of glass and the tree plantings, gives a fluid interpretation of space that relates the large interiors to the landscape. At the front, two smaller cubes project outward from the first floor, one a copper-clad study, the other a glass cube designed to take a suspended sculpture.

Left: **In one of the twin living-rooms, a ten-foot high monolith of granite behind the blue bench occupies part of the large window. A small window cut into the centre also serves as a niche for two glass vases. On the right, a vertical slab of blue onyx supports the surface of a free-standing bar.**

In the same region, close to the burgeoning new business centre of Gurgaon, is a large country estate owned by a successful international businessman. Owning a sculpture by well-known artist Satish Gujral (*see* page 96), he asked Gujral to draw up a design for the estate's buildings using the same style as his sculptures – the artist's first house design.

Above: **Exterior and interior mix as the stone flooring in the living-room changes from slate to grey marble and then extends out to the gardens.**

Far left: **Floating, cantilevered, wooden steps** in the first flight make a deliberate contrast with the monolithic slate mid-landing. The slate from the floor climbs up to this mid-landing, while one of the wooden treads extends to form a ledge, creating an interesting interlocking of materials.

Left: The circular coffee table in this double-height living-room is custom designed and composed of 12 different timbers. All the walls of this room are floor-to-ceiling glass to take advantage of the views of the surrounding estate. The grey sliding screens behind the sofa lead into the dining-room.

Below: Works of art on display in the main living area of the principal house include two paintings by Satish Gujral.

Right: The entrance to each house in the six-villa estate is from the upper level, so that the staircase down plays a prominent role. In the Main House, steps to either side lead to the bedroom floor.

Below right: Light warm colours, austere lines, and rich, natural materials are found throughout. Here, underneath the suspended staircase, the dining area leads onto a small courtyard.

The country estate comprises six villas, of which three are occupied by friends. The other three jointly constitute the main complex; they are built in the form of a semi-circle around a large garden at a lower level, with a swimming pool in its centre. The entrance to each house is accessed from an upper level; a stairway descends to the living-room, dining-room, and kitchen. The bedrooms and bathrooms are on the upper floor. The architectural style is somewhat reminiscent of traditional palaces, with their hanging gardens, inner courts, and arches. The houses are of a symmetrical design and composed of a series of curves. Ten years after their construction, the buildings were in need of renovation, which was undertaken by architect Pradeep Patak and Dutch interior designer Natasja van der Meer. Because the interior structure was so dominant, including hanging stairways, van der Meer decided not to make any major changes. "I decided to adopt an international style for the Main House." In the main living area of the principal house, the overall decoration, as elsewhere, is unpretentious but simultaneously sumptuous, thereby ensuring that full justice is done to the owner's works of art on display. The extremely comfortable furniture is upholstered with natural fabrics such as linen, silk, and wool.

FAMILY EXTENSIONS

Below: **The bathroom is white and minimalist but relieved by a Venetian mirror over the washbasin. The rear wall houses a closed storage unit on the left and white open marble shelves in the centre. To the extreme right is the glass-walled shower cubicle.**

Right: **The study looking out over the rear garden has floor-to-ceiling wood panelling, and a flooring of brown marble tiles.**

Joint family dwellings are one of the most obvious effects of the very communal aspect of Indian home life. When children marry, they tend not to move out, but rather set up a second family unit within the home. Where space allows, this often results in enlargements to the structure, if not in re-allocation and new divisions of the house. In the examples here, the owners have taken the opportunity to create something new in design.

In the first of these extensions, on the outskirts of New Delhi, the new wing projects into the large garden at the rear. With their sons getting married and the family increasing in size, the options were either to build independent houses within the farmland estate or to add additional rooms to the existing house. Wanting to keep the family together while still providing each of their sons with an independent space, they chose to go with the latter. The programme for new extensions involved a complete re-organization of the existing private spaces (bedrooms) on the first floor. The house now has three independent suites, each with two bedrooms (with ensuite bathrooms and dressings) and a living-room for the two sons and the older couple. The ground floor was reorganized to accommodate the formal drawing-room, dining-room, kitchen, an

Below and below centre: The living-room of the extension to the house in Udaipur. The lighting in this room is softened by two devices. One is concealed indirectly behind the large moulded and lacquered white element (below left) that runs around two walls. The other is a soft diffused halo from a suspended glass light tray just below the ceiling (below centre).

informal dining-room and two guest bedrooms. A pool, decking and pavilion were also added in the private garden at the rear.

In the second property, in the Rajasthan city of Udaipur, the original house overlooks one of the several artificial lakes and is a lovely example of a free-standing two-storey dwelling from the 1940s. Its simple lines made it suitable to extend sideways into the tree-bordered garden with a clean modernist wing, built for one of the newly married children. Lighting, as always with Saini, plays an important role in his interiors, for which he pays particular attention to the balance between daylight and artificial light sources and the way in which this balance shifts through the day into the evening. Avoiding fussy window dressing, for the living-room he hung two brown-and-grey Roman blinds, handmade in linen over the two windows that look out onto the garden with its view of the lake. The heavily diffused

light through the fabric is balanced against a long light "tray" of his own design fitted flush to the ceiling above the windows, supported by 50-millimetre (2-inch) thick clear glass brackets anchored in the masonry wall. The 12-millimetre (½-inch) thick sheets of acid-etched glass diffuse the lamps to produce a halo of light for this side of the room.

Opposite, a huge floating bracket in white lacquered wood wraps around two sides of the room. With rounded edges and corners, it serves to articulate the space, to provide two areas of bench seating in an L-shape, and importantly, to carry the concealed lighting. Lighting for the bedroom is an equally considered balance between daylight and artificial. The principal window occupies the corner, with mitred glass panes for simplicity, its height low but extending to the floor so as to exclude the sky from the view – the view of trees and grass gives a softer light.

Below: **The bedroom of the Udaipur extension, looking over a massive marble ledge that curves downwards to form the base of a lounger. A mitred glass corner to the bedroom looks out over the garden.**

Right: In another view of the bedroom, the 75-millimetre (3-inch) thick white marble ledge runs along one wall and turns perpendicular to it to form a desk then lounger. This helps the spatial division of the room, providing a degree of separation between the bed and lounging areas. Two 4.5-metre (15-foot) long photo-montages printed on canvas accentuate the linearity of the marble ledge.

DESIGNER'S APARTMENT

Below: **The high-ceilinged living-room is entered here from a small lobby area that was originally a watchman's bedroom. The sculpture, representing a braid of hair, is by Ravinder Reddy, whose works celebrate Indian woman as "goddess" and explore a playfulness between the ordinariness of day-to-day women's dress and ornaments and an iconic power imbued through monumental proportions.**

American-born designer Michael Aram lives in this ground-floor apartment in one of New Delhi's historically most interesting buildings. Constructed in 1945 by Sir Shoba Singh, who was Lutyen's builder during the grand design for India's new capital, it was designed by Walter George as accommodation for single Britons waiting for their families to join them. Unusually for India, it has tall ceilings, enormously thick walls, and a symmetry broken only by French doors. Aram says, "it is by far the most intelligently designed space I have lived in in India. The space is intimate, yet is great for parties of 100 or more."

When he moved into the apartment, Aram stripped it of all built-ins. "I enjoy keeping the space very open, and treating it in a modern and clean way. At the same time, I love the objects I have collected over the years, and enjoy giving them the room I feel they need to breathe in, rotating them in and out of storage to keep them fresh to the eye." Aram has a particular love of the concept of "ritual objects" and many pieces that had ceremonial functions are displayed alongside his own works (including the cast-bronze "key" door).

Above: The view from the dining-room through to the living-room. The table is set with Aram's designs, including lotus plates hand forged and engraved in stainless steel that are typical of his continuing exploration of natural organic shapes and love of narratives.

Left: One of Aram's designs is this bronze door on a theme of keys. He was attracted to working in India because of "the incredibly rich craft traditions in this country, and was seduced by the possibilities of working with local artisans to forge my artistic vision. I felt liberated working with materials and techniques that were previously difficult to do in New York."

MUMBAI APARTMENTS

Mumbai is the business and entertainment capital of India (and entertainment in the form of movies is a major business) and a highly desirable place to live. It is also running at full occupancy – even after land reclamation, there is nowhere else to build. Land prices in the southern part of the small peninsula, in fashionable districts like Walkeshwar, Malabar Hill, and Colaba, are astronomical by international standards, and while the overall quality of city life measured in cleanliness, air, traffic, and general appearance leaves much to be desired, property values are among the highest on the planet. For almost everyone in Mumbai, home means an apartment.

A desirable location, of course, is everything, and the apartments featured here have it. One, in Walkeshwar, lies below Malabar Hill, overlooking Back Bay with a view towards Nariman Point in the distance. The single, large living area receives all its light from one side – the full-length, sea-facing window. For Rajiv Saini, the designer, this meant employing design strategies that apparently even out the lighting across the room and finding ways of partitioning that would still leave the space feeling open. "Division of space was my main concern here," he remarked, "but before that I had to familiarize myself with the clients' extensive collection of art, principally sculptures and bronzes." The collection heavily influenced the design through the need for display units, lighting, and, most prominently, the basic division. The statue of Mahavir, the 24th and last Jain *tirthankara* – one of that religion's spiritual teachers, the so-called "fordmakers" because, having achieved enlightenment themselves, they founded communities to act as "a ford across the river of human misery" – was chosen to be the focal point of the partition. Although the statue is not large, its characteristic stance – standing with arms straight down at the sides – gives it a commanding presence, particularly in this setting, where it occupies a place in the middle of a room rather than standing in a niche, which would have been its originally intended position.

In the case of a smaller apartment in Worli, Saini took a different initial approach, knowing that he would not have a collection of art to integrate and work with. "I knew in advance that I would have to make a strong statement through the design instead." The apartment is in one of the best-sited buildings in Mumbai, built in the late 1960s on a headland just

Below: **The living-room of the apartment in Walkeshwar features a white marble statue of Lord Mahavir in the centre of a low horizontal linear element clad in metal and pierced with a trough containing marigolds. This low linear division separates the space into two zones without visually blocking one from the other. The saffron-lacquered metal backdrop to the statue forms a visually arresting vertical feature.**

Below: **At the entrance to a new beach-front apartment in Worli. Lacquered partitions separate this space from the main living and dining areas, one of them displaying a greatly enlarged backlit photograph of leaves.**

north of Haji Ali, a small bay in the centre of which is a well-known mosque. The apartment has views out to sea from one side and back towards the bay from the other. The first focus of attention was the entrance hall. Because of the restricted space available (which accommodates a combined living/dining-room and three bedrooms), the owner was concerned to have a lobby as an intermediate space for guests and as a place for removal of shoes (as is customary in India, indeed in most of Asia).

Here Saini aimed for a striking first impression of the apartment by installing two free-standing panels in bright saffron orange, executed in a synthetic lacquer. From the

doorway, the side panel is a single block of colour, while the narrower panel facing the entrance is a large light-box backed with orange. Fluorescent strips backlight a transparent photographic collage, for which several largely abstract photographic images were considered. The photographer recommended the use of leaves because of their auspicious rôle in ritual (in offerings and garlands), which would make them particularly appropriate for the entrance to a home. A pattern of extreme close-ups was finally agreed upon, in warm colours to fit with the panels. Two small but solid wooden stools where guests can sit and remove their shoes complete the small lobby. Conceived by Saini as "tribal" designs, they complement each other as positive and negative forms.

Below: **The reverse of the same partitioned lobby. The sideboard on the dining area side was custom-designed.**

The combined living and dining space, which stretches from the sea-view window back to the kitchen, is animated by contrasting textural surfaces – one wall is formed of bands of stone, while another is clad in pale African walnut. In the rear bedroom, which is used by the owner's elder son, Saini used more semi-abstract photographic imagery as a key element in the design. Above the bed, a long panel features three images of Mumbai streets, all of which have been photographed as reflections in vehicles, including chromework and a car bonnet.

In his own apartment, Saini concentrated on a crisp, clean, and modern conversion in a block on Pali Hill in the suburb of Bandra. Even from these fourth-floor windows, there is abundant greenery visible and Saini did away with curtains and blinds, replacing window frames and using glass-to-glass mitred corners. An important element is a collection of art and antiques. "Most of the antiques," says Saini, "are steeped in mythology and folklore, and have ritualistic associations – and that's what appeals to me, the stories they tell. They also all lean toward folk and tribal traditions, as opposed to the severe and rigid classical forms."

Below: A portrait by Jadish Calla of the architect-owner hangs against a lacquered, white, floor-to-ceiling shutter in the bedroom. Bedside tables have copper frontage and a thick, solid marble detail. A grid of bronzes is inset into the wall above the desk.

COLOUR AND TEXTURE

Below: The Earth Court, the first of four courtyards, is approached along a long, narrow, granite walkway. Plantings include the tulsi, or holy basil, on a blue floor with niches for lights behind, which alludes to the mythological story of Tulsi as the incarnation of a princess who fell in love with Lord Krishna and its rôle in the ritual of the consecration of the *Kalasha*, the container of holy water.

For a two-bedroomed house on the outskirts of Ahmedabad in Gujarat, the owner wanted to integrate the property with the surrounding farmland to maintain a sense of rusticity. The family firm is now in its third generation as a landscape design practice, and the original discussions had been about the landscaping of the site. The owner wanted it left "just wild", but architect Aniket Bhagwat demonstrated the need to consider architecture, interior, and exterior design as a whole. A water body was integral, in the form of a pond surrounded by sedges, and one side of the house was designed to take full advantage of this, with a projecting verandah for viewing and a wooden jetty.

The basic plan is an axis with courts and terraces on either side. Two parallel walls define the axis, forming the long entrance corridor and continuing through the end wall into a courtyard and then up to the landscaped lawn and garden at the far end as an exterior

staircase. This is the spine of the single-storey property and it opens out onto three principal courtyards, each with a different theme that connects to the surrounding natural landscape. For the first, the Earth Court, accessed immediately after entering by means of long, folding, metal doors, Bhagwat chose the most traditional of rustic treatments – cow dung applied by hand in a neat pattern of overlapping curves, renewed every month. The second, the Fragrant Court, features a geometric planting of four varieties of jasmine, which can be enjoyed from the French windows of one bedroom and from a roofed sitting-out area opposite. The third open space, beyond the corridor wall and entered from the living and dining area, is the Water Court, the central feature of which is a stone fountain.

Within this essentially straightforward structure, the house displays a brightness and energy that derives from Bhagwat's use of colours and of different material finishes. "I'm tired of what has become an almost automatic adherence to minimalism," he says. "It has its applications, but too often it simply becomes boring and featureless." In the colour

Below left: **The Water Court, adjacent to the dining space, seen from the continuation of the axis, here open to the sky. A stone fountain splashes water all over the floor.**

Below: **Soil from the pond is banked up alongside the house, providing a flow of levels that help to distinguish the living spaces in vibrant colours from the sombre grey of the entrance tunnel.**

Below: A curved concrete wall marks the end of the walkway. On the other side is a wood and leather seat.

Right: The entrance tunnel, formed of offcut waste from local granite mills, is punctuated with twisted copper-tube lights.

scheme, Bhagwat took a tropical approach reminiscent of the Mexican architects Barragán and Legoretta, using solid washes of primary and secondary colours, each on one wall surface. Despite the Indian love of bright colour in certain aspects of life, this exuberance is generally avoided in homes. He took an equally unconservative approach to the materials, from the steel doors of the corridor to the apparently chiselled granite walls, which are actually waste from the machine-cutting process. The overall result is a house that bursts with ideas, texture, and colour, and yet sits comfortably within its rural surroundings.

BARS AND RESTAURANTS

Below: **A plaster relief wall, inspired by Mughal stone- work, extends into the bar behind. All the furniture has been custom designed by Conran & Partners.**

Below right and far right: **A 12 metre curved wall separates the restaurant from the bar at the Park's Fire and Agni. A triple laminate of acrylic, each sheet carrying a different stylized flame motif, appears to glow and flicker as the lighting cycles between the layers.**

A cosmopolitan approach is taken by the new restaurant-cum-bar in Delhi's Park Hotel. Separated by a curved copper and glass wall, the restaurant, called Fire, and the bar, Agni, were both designed by Conran & Partners (which also worked on another property for the same owners, the Park Hotel in Chennai). In Hindu mythology, Agni is the god of fire, and restaurant and bar present two faces of the same theme. Together, they are also the first stage in a major refurbishment of this city-centre hotel, which will follow the Hindu concept of the Five Elements, the *Panch Maha Bhutas*. These are sky (*Aakaash*), air (*Vaayu*), fire (*Agni*), water (*Jala*), and earth (*Bhuumi*), and each of the various different zones of the hotel will take one of these as its theme.

In Colaba, the southern tip of Mumbai, a couple of blocks from the Gateway of India, chef Rahul Akerkar and his wife, Malini Vachani, opened a restaurant in an old colonial mansion

in 1999. Calling it Indigo, they looked for a modern interior design that would match the
new cuisine, which offers Indian and international dishes, all with an inventive twist. The
first job of architect Bijoy Jain was to bring light into rooms that were lit only from
windows at the front, themselves shaded by trees. The building had already been operating
as a restaurant, but with two rooms occupying what was to become the main dining-room.

Jain had the partition removed and solved the light problem by opening up a skylight
above the centre of one long wall. This became the principal design feature of the
restaurant, in the form of a pool, fed by a spout and pumped water from one side. Jain
made use of Mumbai's strong sunlight by reflecting it and playing with colours. The
interior bay of the pool is in a shade of blue that approaches lapis as closely as possible,
while the water is half covered with fresh floating marigolds. The play of colours from this
classic combination of blue and orange interacts with the large room, which has walls
finished in pale cream. Rather than paint the walls, Jain used the traditional *araish* lime-
plastering technique that he applied also in the apartment featured on pages 18–23.
Pigment is mixed with the marble dust and lime at the stage of plastering for a more
permanent finish than paint would give.

As the sunlight changes throughout the day, the combinations of reflected light and colour provide a steadily changing atmosphere. An open stairwell at the back of the bar, which is connected to the dining-room by two open arches, is a second skylight, with its wall finished in red – a more traditional, highly polished finish in contrast to the textured cream walls on the ground floor. This is an even more time-consuming type of *araish* process, as the surface must be polished with agate – at a maximum rate of 0.58 square metres (6 square feet) per worker per day.

Also in Mumbai are two adjacent new restaurants at the Oberoi hotel, where graphic themes play a key rôle in establishing identity. Frangipani is a contemporary Italian restaurant and here the dominant motif used is Hindi script etched into green-glass panels. A glass wall gives out onto a row of frangipani trees, floodlit at night, and these trees extend past the second restaurant opposite, called India Jones, which serves dishes from a variety of Asian cuisines. Visually, this restaurant is announced by an eclectic mix of artefacts and graphics, including calligraphy – the poems of the seventh-century Chinese poet Li Bai are inscribed on one of the walls.

Below: **At India Jones restaurant in Mumbai, the entrance, with frangipani trees to one side, is dominated by a shallow pool surrounded with lights. In the centre of the pool are three antique Thai temple finials in the form of highly stylized *garuda*, the man-bird from Hindu mythology.**

Top and bottom left: **Hindi** script etched into glass partitions and panels at Frangipani restaurant at the Oberoi, Mumbai, provides a graphic theme that complements the red walls and stainless-steel equipment, such as this pizza oven.

Top right: **At the entrance to the Park Hotel Chennai,** the traditional lotus welcome is re-interpreted by artist Hemi Bawa as giant metal lotus leaves rising from a metal pond.

Bottom right: **At Cilantro restaurant in the Oberoi's Gurgaon hotel,** narrow glass cylinders containing roses are set into a glass wall behind banquette seating.

CITY HOTELS

Below: **Carnations tied with copper wire to large white marble river pebbles float in water-filled glass containers.**

Right: **The orange onyx theme introduced in the lobby is continued in the Onyx bar. The counter-top and two vertical wall-panels (one of them visible on the other side of the wall) are in this local stone.**

The setting of India's first genuinely boutique hotel is as unexpected as its interior conversion. Friends Colony West is one of the gated residential suburbs in southern New Delhi (and, coincidentally, it is also the location of the family home featured on pages 24–9).

The Manor is a two-storey 1950s house that has been converted into an 18-room designer hotel, which opened in 1999. The clean, rectangular lines of the building – one of the better small examples of International Style architecture – lent themselves to the conversion, which on the exterior involved increasing the window area.

The understated décor of the interiors makes a sharp break with all that is normally expected from Indian hotels, which generally tend towards conveying luxury either by stressing history or, more frequently, through excess. The original development of The Manor was conceived and undertaken by London-based Vinay Kapoor and his wife, Shirley Fujikawa, through their company UrbaCon. The result is a type of Indian post-modern, with hints of Art Deco in the clean geometric lines and in the combinations of wooden furniture with chrome, glass, and polished stone.

Shirley took charge of the design, opting for a post-modernist effect but with a colour palette of considerable subtlety, avoiding any of the primary exuberance that is so characteristic of city street-life in India. Additional work was undertaken – but in the same vein of restrained elegance – when the hotel was taken over by the Aman group. Terrazzo flooring is set against white and silvery-grey slate walls, with cherrywood panelling and chrome fittings, while the furniture upholstery is in browns, creams, and similar muted tones.

Following spread: **The inner lobby and corridor of The Manor follow a scheme of white, cream, brown, and grey with contrasting textures of material – terrazzo, wood, and stone. A backlit panel of onyx provides a colour accent.**

convert, with a window on the outer wall and doorways on each of the other three. The only solution was a freestanding bed in the middle, and an imposing Dutch four-poster takes this central position with ease.

Apart from the major work, the Drechsels decided to retain as much as possible of the original detailing, while adding colour and art from their large ethnographic collection. For the paintwork, they chose the traditional Keralan method of lime paint. The base for this is the crushed lime from shells collected in Lake Vembanad and the Backwaters, to which pigment is added. The walls of the living-room, for example, are painted in a blue-turquoise pigment that was once common in the old Muslim quarter of Mattancherry. The ethnographic art pieces in this room include a a fine 18th-century wood-carved Hindu statue in the traditional Kerala style, a boat-shaped wooden bowl that was used for collecting alms in a mosque, and a human-shaped wooden plank that was part of a Christian baptism ritual. The furniture is a mixture of modern and historic, with a replica Dutch trader's chair and an old Brahmin bed used as a table.

Left: The columned entrance porch is guarded by three wooden masks, while the cut-out image of Mahatma Gandhi serves for the owners as a counterweight to the building's colonial history.

Below, left: The main hall was opened up and made lighter and brighter. The wooden water buffalo is from southwestern Karnataka, the bird masks from northern Kerala.

Below right: In a corner of the hall, looking through the arch into the dining area and kitchen door, are two cast-bronze roof finials from a mosque or temple.

ICONS, MOTIFS, FORMS

Above left: **A modern, stylized interpretation of the elephant-headed god Ganesh, highly popular in India as a bringer of good fortune. The stone sculpture is by the artist Satish Gujral.**

Above right: **Michael Aram's collection of ritualistic artefacts includes this folk-art head of a cow, sacred in Indian culture because of its associations with Lord Krishna and Lord Shiva.**

Decoration has always played an important rôle in Indian architecture, and it has certainly not been abandoned in new interiors. As part of the modern design movement, as well as modern Indian art, the iconic forms of tradition and religion are themselves being re-worked and re-interpreted, sometimes playfully, affectionately or as a challenge to old received ideas. The lotus, the cow, and the elephant-headed god Ganesh, to name three examples, are powerful and familiar symbols that lend themselves to new treatment.

The persistence of symbol in Indian design and graphics can be traced back to the still-powerful rôle of religion in normal life. The lotus symbolizes many things, but all connected with birth and creation, whether of knowledge, awareness, or existence. When Vishnu, reclining on the great serpent that floats on the cosmic ocean, dreams the universe into existence, a lotus sprouts from his navel, its flower opening to reveal Brahma. A favourite symbol of Buddhism, it is rooted in mud, rises through water, and opens in sunlight. Since the time of the Gupta dynasty around the 4th to 6th centuries AD, the cow has been a sacred object of veneration, while in the male form is associated with Nandi, the steed of Lord Shiva. Ganesh, the son of Lord Shiva and bringer of wealth and good fortune, is not

Left: Lotuses run as a theme throughout a duplex suite at Devi Garh, designed by Rajiv Saini. Here on the staircase they are carved out of marble and appear in lit paper sculptures that were originally designed for a wedding celebration.

Clockwise, from top left:

The *naga*, derived ultimately from the cobra, is a sacred serpent that features in both Hindu and Buddhist iconography. Here it is abstracted in brass as door handles at the Trident, Gurgaon.

The brass head of a bull on the wall of a modern courtyard recalls Nandin, the steed of Lord Shiva.

Traditional techniques with a modern purpose. Gold leaf applied over a rich blue ground is used for one wall of the library at Vanyavilas at the wildlife sanctuary of Ranthambore, evoking the forests that are still famous for their tiger population.

White silk appliqué lotuses on organza screen a window and echo the silver lotus embroidery on the sofa cushions.

At Vanyavilas, a Tree of Life is interpreted in mirrored glass. This old technique involves hand-blowing spheres of glass, silvering them on the inside, then breaking them into leaf-shaped shards.

Two white marble dishes form the base for a lamp in the apartment of Jivi Sethi, and are a subtle modern interpretation of *pietra dura* inlay, using mother-of-pearl.

The peacock as a royal symbol was used widely in palace decoration, and is here interpreted in a modern fresco by Mohan Singh Kumawat.

Left: The cusped arch, which in its many forms, has become a symbol of Indian architecture, is used here imaginatively to create shelving in a light, airy study in a house in Jaipur.

Below: Carved in stone, another small cusped arch becomes a decorative niche, which holds a marble vase with inlaid malachite strips.

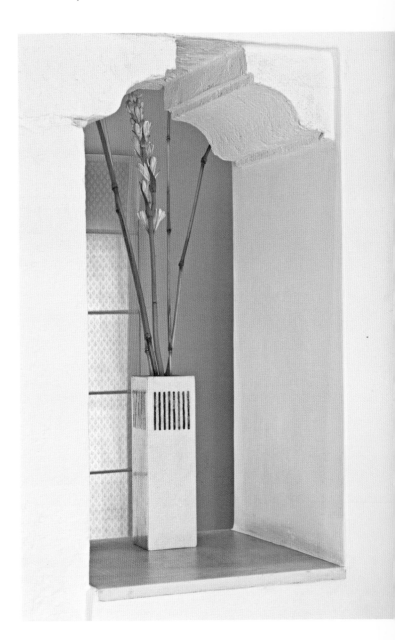

Below and right: **The iconic Ambassador car, symbol of India's post-Independence bootstrap economy. Both pieces are by Subodh Gupta.**

surprisingly popular throughout India, where a large part of the population has good reason to ask for his intercession. These motifs are intensely familiar to all Indians, and also have meaning. At the same time, the iconography has not become regulated, as it has in some other religions. We can see this particularly in the case of Ganesh which, whether treated classically or in the vernacular, has often been rendered idiosyncratically, from hyper-realistically to abstract. As an instantly recognizable form with no prescription, Ganesh and these other icons of Indian life are ideal material for new designs.

All is open to interpretation, and one of the invigorating aspects of India's modern revival in design is the preparedness to play. This extends, naturally, to more modern icons, such as the Ambassador car. This car – made in India and unchanged in design in half a century – is one of the most enduring icons of 20th century India, marking an era of the country's self-sufficiency. In the Poddar house featured on pages 12–17, it is celebrated in two works of art because its manufacture has been one of the family's businesses. A full-sized cast aluminium sculpture by Subodh Gupta stands in the driveway with a real counterpart – one of the family fleet – and a painting by the same artist dominates the study.

.

Chapter 3

Courtyard and Tent

INDIA'S CLIMATE, IN PARTICULAR THE FIERCE HEAT OF ITS SUMMERS, HAS ALWAYS HAD A STRONG INFLUENCE ON ITS ARCHITECTURE. THE PRINCIPAL RESPONSE OF BUILDING DESIGN TO THE HIGH TEMPERATURES, ESPECIALLY IN HOUSES, IS THE COURTYARD, OR *CHOWK*. IT PROVIDES A CENTRAL, SHELTERED, OPEN SPACE THAT, AMONG OTHER THINGS, HELPS TO BLURS THE DISTINCTION BETWEEN INDOORS AND OUTDOORS.

Known by a variety of names in its several regional variations, the courtyard house was probably the most distinctive and widespread vernacular form in Indian architecture. Across the northern plains, including Punjab, Gujarat, Rajasthan, Delhi, and Lucknow, the urban mansion was known as *haveli*, a term that derives from the Arabic *haola*, meaning partition. Typically between two and five storeys, these inward-looking buildings, with their backs firmly closed to the world outside, opened in the centre to a courtyard, around which daily life revolved. In Hyderabad, where the word *haveli* was used for palaces, courtyard houses were called *deori*; in Maharashtra they were *wada*; in Bengal, *rajbari*; while in the south of India their equivalents were *nalukettu* in Kerala and the famous Chettiar merchants' homes in Tamil Nadu. As normal family dwellings they have all but disappeared, but they are now enjoying, in Rajasthan at least, a sort of revival as restored heritage hotels. Essentially, climate helped to create a way of life in which exterior space was naturally assimilated into the interior, and the implications were not only structural and architectural, but also cultural. Another traditional solution is tented space, from awnings to freestanding structures. While the most well-known form of this was the tented encampment for princely hunting parties, the idea has wider expression. Modern design in India is making use of both these forms – courtyard and tent – to extend interiors outwards, allowing buildings to make good use of outdoor space while still retaining privacy.

A NEW HAVELI

Previous spread: **A glass lightbox by Jivi Sethi, at the entrance to a New Delhi courtyard, takes as its design the Tree of Life, which is a recurring theme in Indian design.**

Above: **The view from the main living area on the upper floor towards the balcony, supported by rough-hewn red sandstone pillars.**

Brigitte Singh and her workshop have achieved a special place in the world of Rajasthani textiles. Arriving in India to study miniature painting, she settled, married into a Rajput family, and found the expression of her skills as an artist (and, in particular, colourist) in the design of printed fabrics. Under the guidance of her teacher, and with extensive research over the years into the regional variations of technique and colour, she has taken the traditional woodblock printing, executed by hand, and evolved a predominantly floral design idiom. The workshop, staffed by a hand-picked team of skilled artisans, exports all of its production, most of it to just nine international clients. Now a naturalized Indian citizen, Brigitte Singh is acknowledged within Rajasthan and the country for her contribution to the craft.

With her life and work thoroughly intertwined, Singh decided to design a property that would allow a harmonious relationship between these two aspects of her life. As in her textile designs, in which she draws freely but idiosyncratically on Rajasthani forms and filters them through her own ideas as an artist, the inspiration and materials for the house, Narad Ka Bagh, are also local-yet-adapted. She typically relied on her own sense of appropriate space rather than employ an architect, and chose as her model a kind of modern *haveli*. As noted earlier (*see* page 24), these traditional large homes are shielded to the surroundings and open up centrally – ideal for the communal life of a design workshop. Completed in 1995 on the outskirts of Amber, north of Jaipur, the building revolves around a central, but unusually asymmetrical, courtyard, with a single tree growing in the middle. The ground floor is where she and her team create the textiles, while the upper floor houses the living quarters. A perimeter of simple, red-sandstone pillars around this courtyard support the balcony and the open roof. Although connected by the courtyard, the two levels have different spatial and lighting qualities. The courtyard is the light well and hub for the busy and animated workshop, while the living floor is calmer and more open, with the large living and dining space opening to the exterior garden through windows and balcony along two sides, as well as to the court on the other. This is the focus of the living quarters, and in its arrangement of furniture, striking floor tiling in a black-and-white chevron design, and the internal reflections of the bright sunlight, it adds an almost Provençal atmosphere to the Rajasthani architectural elements.

Below: **Seen from the opposite side of the balcony, the perimeter of the balcony over the courtyard is trapezoidal rather than the conventional rectangular.**

Right: **Niches of different shapes and depths are let into the walls of all the rooms and corridors. One of a series of carved and painted birds accompanies two glass vases.**

Below right: **A simple wooden chair is upholstered with one of the fabrics designed by Brigitte Singh and produced in the workshop below.**

Far right: **Steps set into the pale yellow wall of the living area, leading up to a roof terrace, echo the strong chevron design of the floor, in black-and-white tiles.**

COURTYARD, VERANDAH, GARDEN

Above: A "Tree of Life" light-box designed by Jivi Sethi stands at the entrance to the courtyard.

Right: The spa at Rajvilas (*see* pages 80–1) has a covered extension that creates a sitting-out area. A Tree of Life fresco adorns one wall.

Following spread: At the Sethi apartment in one of New Delhi's colonies, high walls convert the chevron-tiled terrace into a courtyard, which is used largely for entertaining.

The traditional courtyard, or *chowk*, is open to many interpretations, but the constant principles of all are that they should provide shelter from the sun, coolness, privacy, and a space for communal interaction (indeed, *chowk* is also applied in a public context to village squares and crossroads). In former domestic Indian architecture it allowed private enjoyment of the open air and, more than that, served as a kind of regulator for the seasons. As T.S. Randhawa writes in his definitive study *The Indian Courtyard House*, "The courtyard ordered other spaces in an abode where space was not rigidly fixed but could be adaptable depending on the time of day, season, and exigency. It obliquely controlled the environment inside and served the needs of its inhabitants. Its moods changed with varying degrees of light and shade, and with them the ambience of the abode. Centrally located, it imprinted the domain of the dwelling like a visual anchor." A more specific expression in Hindi is *aangan*, the inner courtyard that is traditionally a female domain.

Below: **A statue of Ganesh in an over-sized niche marks the transition between a corridor leading from the Udaipur house featured on pages 40–43 and an interior courtyard. Polished brown Jaisalmeer stone contrasts with strips of graphic black and white tiling.**

Here the women would share household work, clean vegetables, and tend the children. Such an inner courtyard would often have included a tulsi (holy basil) tree, to which prayers were offered. It was, as Randhawa puts it, "the spatial, social, and environmental control centre of the house".

All of these traditional functions demonstrate the flexibility of this way of ordering space, and modern architects and interior designers have been quick to adapt these principles to the different needs of today in their designs for contemporary courtyards. One key use is in articulating the totality of habitable space, whether in a private residence or in a more public structure such as a hotel. At the Trident Gurgaon (*see* pages 84–7), landscape

architect Pui Phornprapha explains that a key purpose was to "create silence and tranquillity inside by using the principle of courtyard ... in order to facilitate potent internal tranquillity in contrast to the undesirable force of urbanism."

While a single courtyard is highly effective in preserving a calm and essentially private space from a crowded, public environment, a sequence of courtyards can work even more powerfully. In the case of the Gurgaon property, the sequence is geometrically structured from the motor court onwards, using the principle of the *mandala*. With each courtyard separated visually from the next, the linear experience of arrival proceeds from chaos (amply provided by the modern city) to order and calm at the centre of the complex.

Below: The courtyard itself, paved with rough local sandstone, features an angled screen clad with reddish sandstone and containing a water spout in the form of a brass cow's head. The screen's purpose is to conceal the kitchen windows behind, while offsetting it from the rear wall allows ample light and ventilation for the kitchen – a modern version of the *modh* or baffle wall that gives visual protection to a traditional house.

Far left: Verandahs, courtyards, and terraces interlock in the house of Faith and John Singh, on the outskirts of Jaipur. The local red sandstone is used here for flooring, bench, and balcony.

Left: At Devi Garh (*see* pages 68–73), landscape architect Aniket Bhagwat introduced trees – here a banana tree – into the *aangan*, or inner women's courtyards, as well as rough-hewn local stone boulders, this one cut into a monumental seat.

Another threshold space is the verandah – *barandah* in Hindi – and the related *otla* in Gujarati, which is a raised platform in front of an entrance that serves to connect interior and exterior. At the house of John and Faith Singh, near Jaipur, set among mango trees, a modern interpretation of the verandah is used throughout the cluster of buildings to create outward-looking interiors with views of the small ponds and gardens.

The traditional courtyard was so much in practical use as to leave little or no room for display – which is to say designating an area, much less an entire court, to be admired visually rather than entered. The latter idea draws more on East Asian theories of garden design, but has now entered the vocabulary of modern Indian courtyard and verandah spaces. The Geometric Court at Gurgaon is one such example, recessed to one side of the main axis in a large bay. Another is the template of bathroom gardens designed for Rajvilas in Jaipur (*see also* pages 80–1). These small planted areas are backed by high walls for privacy and are separated from each bathroom by only a full-height, frameless window.

Right: **Plate-glass windows and large mirrors give protected yet open bathing from sunken marble tubs at Vanyavilas, with a view onto walled private gardens.**

Left: The Geometric Court at Gurgaon, set between the Motor Court and the Main Entrance Court, was conceived by designer Pui Phornprapha with a chequerboard pattern of white river stone and wedelia underneath a frangipani trees to "provide passers-by with simple warmth and peace".

Above: **On the verandah, one of two facing, wooden swings and a blue, translucent column. Mirror fragments inlaid in the terrazzo floor catch and reflect a continuous dance of light. Beyond, in the garden, a fibreglass column impressed with the forms of shells becomes illuminated in the evening.**

Following spread: **The living-room, looking through to a court formed by the entrance wall. The doors and windows carry transparent photographs of coconut palms, sandwiched between glass, so that when the doors are shut, silhouettes of the trees encompass the space. The far wall is imprinted with champa leaves and painted in gold.**

onto a terrace facing the shore. Steps lead up the outside of the house to an extensive roof terrace, which provides even better views.

The labour-intensiveness of the Indian construction industry allowed the entire commission to be executed in three and a half months from the first concept sketches. Because of the lack of mass-production and machine-made elements, and the complete reliance on pairs of hands, it was possible to complete the full range of building and design activity in parallel and at outstanding speed. Provided that the artisans can be efficiently sourced, even unreasonable schedules can be met by throwing more workers at a project.

The highly individual, themed character of the beach house was made possible by the ease of making everything locally – and sometimes on the spot. As Aniket describes it, "Except for the fans and the toilets, everything was made to order for the house. That included furniture, door-handles, lights, window-frames – every major structural element and tiny detail... And the speed at which this happened was phenomenal. Often we would have a meeting early in the morning with the fabricators – carpenters, metal worker, or whoever – give them the designs we'd been working on the night before, and by the end of the day they would be back with a mock-up or prototype."

Left: The entrance walkway is a tunnel that leads from land to sea, with the house on either side of it. Three large, circular cut-outs are edged with cast-iron rings that carry the impression of ropes in tension, to give an echo of loading jetties. The wall-plastering carries the imprint of wooden packing-crate stencils.

Below: The orange wall of one of the two sea-facing bedrooms is textured with fish nets imprinted in the plaster. The wall-lights are made of shells mounted on curved wood, while set into the far wall a small aquarium takes the place of a window to the garden.

WEEKEND PAVILION

The district of Alibag, a 40-minute boat ride across the bay from Mumbai, has since the early 1990s become a fashionable upmarket location for weekend homes. Although a part of the mainland – a slow 10-hour drive south will take you to Goa – it is still relatively isolated from the city. Normal housing developments are out of the question because of Mumbai's position at the end of a long peninsula, which makes for a three-hour drive. The pleasure boats that ply from the jetties alongside the Gateway of India, however, are ideal for small numbers of passengers. Beach-front property prices have soared, although there has been little visible impact of new villas – the district is large enough to absorb the newcomers and life goes on as it always has. The mainstays of the local economy are rice and fishing (the best of the catch going daily to Mumbai's markets and restaurants).

Bijoy Jain, already a resident of Alibag for seven years, has a number of ongoing projects for city clients. This, one of the first to be completed, is for a family who wanted open-air living for the two days a week that they regularly use it, including during the monsoon, when the rains are torrential but the countryside is washed clean and bursts into green. The climate, which varies during the year between very warm and very hot, makes this practical.

Below: **Looking along the axis of the pavilion structure of the house. This open area, with a cool, red-sandstone floor and projecting tile roof, is the principal living space, while the bedrooms and utilities are placed in the two rear corners.**

Jain designed the house as a large pavilion with small, attached courtyards, one of which serves as a screen to the access road for the central open area. Pillars support a wide timber roof clad with reddish Mangalore tiles. These well-known roofing tiles are exposed to view to reveal their distinctive decorative patterns and were laid in two layers, the inner one serving to conceal the overlaps of the outer tiles and also to aid insulation against the heat. The brief also called for low-cost construction, which encouraged Jain to rely not only on local craftsmen, but also on the limitations and strengths of their normal work. To this end, he began the project by talking at length to the artisans involved to discover what they could do rather than complicating matters by pushing them to execute unfamiliar specifications. This approach determined many aspects of the building's specifications, for instance the length of timber spans. Nearly all the materials, from timber to olive-green sandstone, were sourced locally. The exception was the principal flooring of red Agra sandstone, and this was chosen for cost reasons as much as for its attractive colour and matte finish – it was part of an unfulfilled order at the Mumbai stone merchants and so was offered at a good price.

Above: The living and verandah spaces open onto each other for a free circulation of air and people. The view through these two doorways is toward a small attached water court, which is backed by a high wall.

A NATURAL SITE

Below: **At the rear of the house, an austere dining-room, simply furnished with floor-level seating, looks onto a small interior court. One of the property's existing trees penetrates the roof.**

When Mumbai architect Samira Rathod first drove to Karjat to inspect the site for this weekend country house, she realized immediately that the tranquillity of the 2.4-hectare (6-acre) property would determine her treatment. The district, a two-hour drive and 85 kilometres (53 miles) from south Mumbai, lies at the foot of the Karjat Hills and is so far largely unspoiled by development. This is probably the closest area of natural scenic beauty to the city and popular for trekking; there are also a number of health farms dotted around. The property's defining feature is a small lake surrounded by trees, visited by waterbirds. The site had already been prepared and levelled before Rathod began work. "I knew that the house had to fit into the natural surroundings so as not to disturb the wildlife," she said, "and it should carry an atmosphere of calm." The client, Sangita Kathiwada, of Mélange fashion house in south Mumbai, and the owner of the property, her uncle Kamal Morarka, wanted a single-bedroomed house that she could use as a peaceful retreat.

Rathod takes a deliberately contextual approach in her work, responding to specific features of different sites. A clear example of this here is the line of three trees a few metres apart, which she integrated into the house, one in an interior courtyard and two on the terrace. This led naturally to an L-shaped plan, with the small courtyard in the angle. The larger, gabled unit faces the lake, while a lower, flat-roofed unit housing the dining-room and kitchen sits at right angles behind. House and trees interpenetrate through two devices. One is framing, which plays an important rôle throughout the design, motivated in part by the client's insistence on a rectilinear treatment, meaning no skewed angles. A rectangular pattern of walls, windows, and interior openings incorporates carefully organized, framed views of the three trees.

The second device is the projection of terraces and balconies into the mid-levels of the trees in front of the house. One of these is a deck that extends the living-room with a lovely view of the lake, the distant hills, and the sunset. Large windows slide back to open the room. The other projection, at a slightly higher level, with branches and leaves within touching distance, extends from the bedroom. The colours used in the house are in tune with the surroundings – soft, muted greens and browns, set off in the small courtyard against one matte black wall. The spare, almost austere treatment of space and use of colour gives an easy sense of living with nature.

Above: **The living-room, which looks out over the trees and lake, is decorated in natural earth colours, including rust, ochre, and maroon, complementing the brown Mandana stone flooring. Floor-to-ceiling glass partitions can slide right back into the walls.**

Following spread: **The bedroom window also slides back completely so that the space projects out and into the trees that grow by the edge of the lake. As throughout the rest of the house, the furniture and lights were designed by the architect as individual works of art, breaking away, in her own words, "from the conventional norms of 'form follows function'".**

NAILA FORT

Possibly the ultimate in private retreats is the hill-top fort at Naila, a little to the east of Jaipur. The fort occupies the summit of an isolated hill and was built as a garrison to defend the village by Thakur of Naila in the 19th century. Eventually deserted, it was bought by Biki Oberoi; although structurally sound, it was totally dilapidated. Architects Prabhat Patki Associates, working alongside Mr Oberoi, began reconstruction in 1986. The work continued over the next several years, during which time the Indian Government declared it a heritage site. The responsibility for designing the 52 rooms and planting the 7.3 hectares (18 acres) of garden fell to Mirjana Jojic-Oberoi. Her vision was a fusion of Eastern and European, for which she scoured the markets of India, the Far East, Africa and Europe, acquiring the brass-studded main gate to the fort, Baccarat lights, Egyptian folding chairs, Victorian bath tubs, among others. Terracotta pots and hand-woven fabrics were made locally, and she designed soft furnishings, air-conditioning covers, up-lighters and much else, including a mirror mosaic ceiling for the Indian Dining Room Turret, inspired by the Room of Mirrors at Amber Fort.

Left: **The circular towers typical of fortification in this part of Rajasthan have been converted into living space. This one (visible in the photograph above in the distance) has a series of traditional brass lamps hanging at varying heights. Light from the tapering, downward-looking archers' windows is supplemented by a larger window at left.**

Above: **The arched areas that separate the row of courtyards from each other are for relaxation. Here they are furnished with colonial planters' chairs.**

A VIEW OF THE HILLS

Below: **A large jacuzzi has been sunk into the crenellated roof of one of the circular tower fortifications, which has a commanding (formerly defensive) view of the hills to the southwest.**

Right: **The Devi Garh suite has a 360-degree view and is equipped with its own outdoor jacuzzi in a marble bathtub, located in a roof-top cupola. Traditional roller blinds –** *chics* **– allow privacy.**

Following spread: **Another marble bathtub is set into the floor of one of the suites and faces a floor-to-ceiling window looking out over a magnificent view of the Aravali Hills.**

Devi Garh, introduced in Chapter 2 (*see* pages 68–73), was re-designed and re-purposed from a Rajput fort into a luxury retreat. This transformation involved more than simply creating stylish suites in the interior of the building. There needed to be a spa with such associated fittings as jacuzzis, and above all, it meant opening up Devi Garh to the stunning exterior views considerably more than would be normal for a fortified structure. There were already a number of small projecting balconies in the *zharooka* style offering spectacular views, and these were converted for use as small rooms for dining and drinking cocktails.

Part of the upper ramparts are also used for yoga (for control of body, breath and mind) and *dhyana* (meditation) at sunrise. In one of the palace suites, which uses silver as its theme and is one of the highest in the fort, the conversion created a large marble bathroom with a sunken bath that has a spectacular wall-to-ceiling framed view of the hills to the south. Two exterior pools-with-views were also added: one a private jacuzzi over the principal, Devi Garh, suite, the other a large circular jacuzzi for all guests built into one of the circular crenellated towers, adjacent to the swimming pool.

DESIGN FOR SPAS

Above: **Close by the old building at Rajvilas that was converted into a spa, a mature neem tree (*Azadirachta indica*) stood. Native to India, this relative of the mahogany is widely relied on for herbal medicine and for use in cosmetic and pharmaceutical products. The designers appropriately incorporated it into this new treatment room added as an extension.**

Right: **The small interior step pool at Vanyavilas. The fresco on the wall beyond is on the theme of the Tree of Life.**

Spas are now an integral part of resort retreats internationally and very much so in India with its long tradition of a holistic approach to wellness and medicine. The indigenous and traditional system of medicine is Ayurveda, meaning "the science of longevity", which is at least 5,000 years old – an accumulation of knowledge with various distinguishing features, including an approach that looks for the balance between three *dosha* or humours.

This holistic approach to wellness, in which the surroundings are considered, gives a special importance to the architecture and interior design of spas. At Rajvilas (*see* pages 80–1), for example, a restored Rajasthani mansion has been converted into spa suites and treatment rooms that overlook private gardens, with an existing, mature neem tree incorporated into the structure – it grows through one of the suites. At Vanyavilas in Ranthambore (*see* pages 82–3), the spa is located over a lake stocked with carp. Nearby, at the tented encampment of Aman-I-Khas (*see* pages 126–31), one over-size tent has been designed as a treatment area for massage, scrubs, and traditional henna application.

Previous spread: **One of the private therapy suites at Vanyavilas in Ranthambore, where a free-standing tub overlooks the lake.**

Opposite page and this page, bottom: **Two views of a treatment room in the Spa Tent at Aman-I-Khas, which features twin massage tables.**

Top left: **At Aman-I-Khas, one of a collection of old Rajasthani bronze jars, or** *kalash*, **has been integrated into a fountain. Water overflows down onto a bed of pebbles.**

Top right: **Neem leaves cover the water in a spa tub at Rajvilas. One of the Meliaceae family, the evergreen neem tree has for centuries been used widely in Indian traditional medicine for various therapeutic purposes.**

SERENITY AND PRIVACY

Below: As evening falls
over Lake Vembanad,
candles are lit around the
verandah of Privacy.
Keralan wooden pillars
support the tiled roof, and
the terracotta sculpture on
the edge of the lake
depicts Lord Rama, his wife
Sita and brother Laxman.

Jörg Drechsel, who re-designed the interiors of the two Fort Cochin houses featured on pages 88–95, also took over two country properties in Kerala to create what he calls "escapes". One is a 1920s plantation house in the foothills of the Western Ghats, the other a converted shed looking out over Lake Vembanad on the Keralan Backwaters. Both are for guests of the Malabar House Residency in Fort Cochin (*see* pages 88–91).

The plantation house, called Serenity, is a two-storey building on the Kanam estate in Kottalam district, where the hills begin to rise towards the Western Ghats, which form the major divide and watershed of southern and southern-central India. The principle here was minimum interference and the use of natural materials, which include coir matting as

floor coverings (coir is derived from coconuts and is one of the area's most profitable products) and handmade paper shades for the lanterns.

Simplicity is also maintained in the design of the lakeside "escape", called Privacy. Lake Vembanad, south of Cochin, is the focus of the Kerala Backwaters, a vast network of rivers and canals that for centuries have offered sheltered southward passage – and were used by Roman and Arabic traders dealing in spices. The location is one of the best on the lake, with a wonderful view across to Kumarakom and the sailing route for the many small fishing boats, yet it is just a few kilometres from the main road. Partly because of the growing tourist boom and development around the lake, new construction on the lake front is now restricted, so Drechsel acquired an existing small property. The building was formerly used as a simple storage shed for shells, which are

Below: **The interior of the small lakeside cottage is furnished with rustic simplicity and clean pastel colours. This is one of the two bedrooms.**

Above: **In the main bedroom of the converted planter's house, the headboard is an old window with the glass panels replaced by mirrors.**

Right: **The staircase at Serenity, its original dark wood lightened by a wash of pale turquoise.**

collected locally in large quantities in order to make lime mortar and lime paint. The shells are first burnt and then crushed into powder – indeed the paint used in The Parsonage (*see* pages 92–5) comes from this traditional source. The interior was completely rebuilt to provide two bedrooms, washrooms, and a central space for dining that opens out to the verandah. This addition, with traditional bulbous Keralan wooden pillars supporting the roof extension, is the highlight of the cottage and its principal living area. The traditional thatching was maintained for the roof.

Index

Page numbers in *italics* refer to picture captions

Acknowledgments

Michael Freeman would like to thank the following for their assistance in creating this book:

Michael Aram

Aniket Bhagwat & Smruti Prabakar

Jayshree Bhartia

Jonathan Blitz and the staff at Aman-I-Khas, Ranthambore

Mathar "Lek" Bunnag

Ruthon and Ellie Chadha

Amrita Jhaveri and Chris Davidge

Suzanne Dawson

Apoorva Desai

The management and staff at Devi Garh

Trina Dingler Ebert

Jean-Michel Gathy

Benoit Ghesquiere-Dierickx and the staff at The Manor, Delhi

Joerg and Txuku Drechsel

Xenia Hohenlohe

Bijoy and Priya Aswani Jain

Mirjana Jojic-Oberoi

Munnu Kasliwal

Sangita Kathiwada and Kamal Morarka

The management and staff at Malabar House, Fort Cochin

Natasja van der Meer

Vikram Oberoi

The management and staff at the following Oberoi properties: Delhi, Vanyavilas (Ranthambore), Udaivilas (Udaipur), Rajvilas (Jaipur), Mumbai, Gurgaon, MV Vrinda.

Pradeep and Anshu Patak

Nimish Patel & Parul Zaveri

Priti and Priya Paul

Stephane Paumier

Lekha, Ranjan and Anupam Poddar

Pui Pornprapha

Samira Rathod

Rajiv Saini

Ingo Schweder

Sekhri family

Jivi Sethi

Rajeev Sethi

The management and staff at Sherbagh, Ranthambore

Brigitte Singh

Faith Singh

Mala Singh

Bina Singhal

Madhu Singhal

Mukul Singhal

Vinita Singhania

Marie-Helène de Taillac

Malini Vachani-Akerkar & Rahul Akerkar at Indigo Restaurant

Deepak Vaidya

Rujiraporn Pia Wanglee